THE SECRET OF THE SCUBA DIVING SPIDER ... AND MORE!

BY ANA MARÍA RODRÍGUEZ

Enslow Publishing
101 W. 23rd Street
Suite 240
New York, NY 10011
USA

enslow.com

Acknowledgments
The author expresses her immense gratitude to all the scientists who
have contributed to the Animal Secrets Revealed! series. Their comments and
photos have been invaluable to the creation of these books.

Published in 2018 by Enslow Publishing, LLC.
101 W. 23rd Street, Suite 240, New York, NY 10011

Library of Congress Cataloging-in-Publication Data

Names: Rodríguez, Ana María, 1958- author.
Title: The secret of the scuba diving spider... and more! / Ana María Rodríguez.
Description: New York : Enslow Publishing, 2018. | Series: Animal secrets revealed! |
Includes bibliographical references and index. | Audience: Grades 3 to 6.
Identifiers: LCCN 2017005212| ISBN 9780766086296 (library bound) | ISBN
9780766088504 (pbk.) | ISBN 9780766088443 (6 pack)
Subjects: LCSH: Insects--Juvenile literature. | Spiders--Juvenile literature.
| Bats--Juvenile literature. | Animal behavior--Research--Juvenile literature.
Classification: LCC QL467.2 .R654 2017 | DDC 595.7--dc23
LC record available at https://lccn.loc.gov/2017005212

Printed in the United States of America

To Our Readers: We have done our best to make sure all websites in this book were
active and appropriate when we went to press. However, the author and the publisher
have no control over and assume no liability for the material available on those websites or
on any websites they may link to. Any comments or suggestions can be sent by email to
customerservice@enslow.com.

Photo Credits: Cover, pp. 3 (top left), 6 Stefan Hetz/Cover of *Journal of Experimental
Biology* July 1, 2011, http://jeb.biologists.org/content/214/13.cover-expansion; pp. 3 (top
right), 15 © Melinda Fawver/Dreamstime.com; pp. 3 (center left), 20, 23 Aaron Corcoran;
pp. 3 (bottom right), 28, 29 Tom Murray; pp. 3 (bottom left), 34 © Chainat/Dreamstime.
com; p. 7 © Dmitry Zhukov/Dreamstime.com; p. 9 © Mishkacz/Dreamstime.com; p. 12
Ana M. Rodríguez; p. 13 © Cpaulfell/Dreamstime.com; p. 17 © Steve Byland/Dreamstime.
com; p. 21 Ken Bennett; p. 27 © Alptraum/Dreamstime.com; p. 30 Cedric Figueres; pp. 35,
37, 39 Tom Libby, Kaushik Jayaram, and Pauline Jennings. Courtesy of PolyPEDAL Lab UC
Berkeley.

★ CONTENTS ★

★

ENTER THE WORLD OF ANIMAL SECRETS

n this volume of Animal Secrets Revealed!, you will join scientists in the field or the lab and discover intriguing adaptations that help animals survive in their environments. You will begin in Germany, diving alongside the only spider capable of living most of its life underwater. Your next adventure will take you to Canada, where you will learn about a caterpillar's emergency whistle. Then, you will visit scientists in the United States, some who spend their nights listening to bats "jamming" for food and others who discovered that zombies—zombie beetles, that is—really exist. Your journey will end with scientists who uncovered the secret of the unstoppable cockroach, which inspired them to build robots that one day may save people's lives.

Welcome to the world of animal secrets!

1
THE SECRET OF THE SCUBA DIVING SPIDER

Roger Seymour and Stefan Hetz, animal biologists, are scouting Germany's northern countryside for the one-of-a-kind diving bell spider, the only spider that lives underwater. It's not an easy search considering that these dark-colored spiders are only as long as one to three grains of rice (0.3 to 0.7 inches, or 8 to 19 millimeters). Under the summer sun, Seymour and Hetz stare patiently into ponds and calmed river shores. They are looking for clues of the spider's presence—the shimmering silvery lining of mini-air bubbles trapped under dome-shaped webs spun between underwater vegetation.

"The diving bell spider is becoming very rare throughout Europe and Asia, mainly because of loss of natural habitats and pollution," Seymour said. "In Germany, they are so rare that they are protected. We needed a permit to collect them."[1]

The diving bell spider weaves a silvery net underwater that envelops an air bubble large enough for the spider to spend more than a day below the surface. Here, the spider is inside a bubble, eating a water flea.

6

Seymour and Hetz found some spiders in the Eider River. They brought these spiders to Hetz's lab at Humboldt University in Berlin where the scientists had aquariums ready. They placed a few strands of water weed inside the aquariums so the spiders could build their diving bells, which are dome-shaped webs that can hold trapped air. The water was at room temperature and did not circulate much—just as the spiders like it. The scientists fed them insect larvae, and the spiders made the aquariums their home. Some of the spiders shed their exoskeletons and others laid eggs in cocoons inside their diving bells.[2]

Spiders living on land build their webs in a variety of places, such as between plant twigs, to trap prey. The scuba diving spider also traps prey by building its web between underwater twigs but has to add a diving bell to breathe.

How a Spider Builds a Diving Bell

Although they are air-breathing animals, diving bell spiders live practically all their lives underwater. They have solved the problem of needing a constant supply of air. They use the hairs on their fuzzy abdomen to trap a layer of air. Then, the spiders take in oxygen from the bubbles covering their abdomen. The spiders also build a diving bell underwater. How this diving bell worked, however, was a mystery until Seymour and Hetz came along.

> **Science Tongue Twister:
> The scientific name for
> the diving bell spider is
> *Argyroneta aquatica*,
> which means "aquatic
> spinner of silver."**

Seymour had been fascinated by the diving bell spider mystery since he was a young child. "When I was about ten years old, someone gave me the book *Curious Creatures* by Erna Pinner," Seymour said. "One of the chapters described the diving bell spider that lived in ponds in Europe. I imagined what it would be like to live inside an underwater bubble held in place by webs. That image remained in my mind until I became a scientist and measured the amount of oxygen diving insects carry in a bubble down with them."[3]

One day at a scientific conference on insects, Seymour, who lives in Australia, met Hetz and asked him whether he had ever found diving bell spiders in Germany. Hetz said that he had seen them. "I proposed that we measure how much oxygen is in the diving bell of the underwater spider," said Seymour. "Nobody had done that before."[4]

8

In Hetz's lab, the spiders were building their underwater webs overnight. They spun silky webs on underwater vegetation. Then, to create the diving bell, the spiders rose to the surface and exposed their abdomen to the air, trapping an air bubble with their hind legs and the hairs on their surface. Back underwater, the spiders released the bubble under the domed web that holds it in place.[5]

"In the morning, we carefully measured the amount of oxygen inside the diving bell with a fiber optic oxygen probe called an optode," Seymour said. "When a spider was present in the diving bell, we saw that the amount of oxygen decreased. When the spider was not in the bell, the oxygen went up, because it came in through the web from dissolved oxygen in the water. This was the first demonstration that the web acted like a gill, exchanging oxygen with the water around it. We then played with different sized bubbles and different sized spiders."[6]

In their underwater shelter, the spiders go about their daily, spidery activities. They capture insects and fish that run into their

Spiders practice the wait-and-catch strategy to capture prey. This striped spider is very still as it waits for its breakfast to get trapped on the sticky, morning-dew web.

A UNIQUE SPIDER

"What I enjoyed the most about studying the underwater spider is that no other spider makes a web underwater, fills it with air, and lives inside it," Seymour said. "I specialize in studying unique and therefore unusual animals and plants. If I had the chance, I would study every one of the animals I saw in *Curious Creatures* as a boy."[9]

underwater silk lines. They also shed their exoskeletons to grow, lay eggs, and raise their young. After a few days with mom, baby diving bell spiders leave and build their own diving bells. Newly hatched spiders make bells the size of the head of a pin, while adults build them the size of your thumbnail. The whole spider can fit inside it.[7]

A Home Underwater

Seymour and Hetz still had more questions about the diving bell spider. How long can it stay in its diving bell? The scientists were surprised that the answer was more than a day! The diving bell eventually shrinks, forcing the spider to take more trips to the surface to refill the air in the bell.[8]

This unique, quiet lifestyle has worked out well for the spiders. It allows them to remain out of sight from predators and create an underwater home where they can grow and reproduce.

2
A CATERPILLAR'S EMERGENCY WHISTLE

ayne Yack, an insect biologist, is savoring an early morning breakfast at home. Suddenly, she hears an unexpected sound. Curious, she interrupts her meal and looks for the sound's source. The sound leads her to the caterpillars she is raising in her house. She looks closer into the caterpillar cage. The caterpillars are making the sounds![1]

This was the first time that Yack had heard caterpillars using sound to communicate with each other. In this case, she heard the larva, or caterpillar, of a hook-tip moth drumming and scraping its mandibles against the surface of a leaf. The caterpillar seemed to be making the sounds to defend its territory from another hook-tip caterpillar who was trying to invade its leaf.[2]

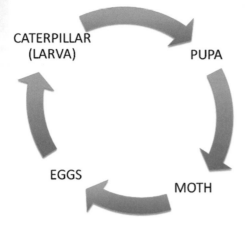

LIFE CYCLE OF A MOTH

The life of a moth starts with an egg that grows into a larva, or caterpillar. The caterpillar then becomes a pupa, a quiet creature that transforms into the final moth. The moth lays eggs, and the cycle of life begins again.

Yack was surprised and intrigued. She knew that many adult insects make sounds—think of crickets chirping or cicadas singing—but young insects, such as caterpillars? That was news. What were the sounds for?

"For about thirty years, I have studied how insects use sound to communicate," Yack said. "I learned that insects use bizarre and abundant sounds and vibrations to talk to each other and with other animals. I wanted to know what the sounds of caterpillars mean."[3]

The Not-So-Quiet Caterpillar

Caterpillars have a long list of predators. Birds, mice, bats, snakes, frogs, beetles, spiders, and other animals all have caterpillars on their menus. In response, caterpillars, quiet as they may seem, can counter their predators' attacks in a number of ways.

Caterpillars' first defense is usually to hide. They can hide under leaves. Some caterpillars have colors that match

Many animals eat caterpillars. But the green color of a walnut sphinx moth larva helps it blend in with its environment—tree branches and leaves—and escape predators.

those of their surroundings. This camouflage makes it difficult for hungry predators to find them. However, when predators find them, caterpillars have more in their bag of tricks to escape from becoming a meal. Some caterpillars have spines and hairs that sting, sometimes with chemicals predators don't like. Other caterpillars wear colors that warn predators of poisons inside the caterpillar's body.[4]

On occasion, caterpillars resort to deceit. For instance, some hawkmoth caterpillars have a pattern on their body that looks like eyes. When attacked, these caterpillars move their head into their chest, which makes the "eyes" look bigger, and this scares predators. Some caterpillars get physical. They can spit stuff at predators, thrash, or bite.[5]

That morning during breakfast, Yack realized that the caterpillars' bag of escape tricks has more than just looks and moves. Caterpillars of the hook-tip moth can also make sounds to discourage others of its kind to come to their territory. Yack was curious. What other sounds can caterpillars make? She decided to investigate.

When Caterpillars Are Under Attack

Jayne Yack, Veronica Bura, and their colleagues discovered that some caterpillars whistle. Birds can hear some of the whistles. Other whistles are ultrasonic, outside what a bird can hear, but might be heard by other animals.

To investigate whether caterpillar whistles could be a kind of defense against an attack, the researchers first went to Lake Opinicon in Canada. There, at Queens University Biological Station, the scientists captured walnut sphinx moths by attracting them to ultraviolet light. They harvested the eggs of the moths. Then, the scientists reared the caterpillars on twigs of walnut or beech, some of the caterpillar's favorite plants.[6]

The scientists hypothesized that if larvae use whistling as a defense, they will whistle when they are under attack. To test their hypothesis, Yack, Bura, and their colleagues set up two separate experiments. During the experiments, the researchers recorded the sounds with microphones and other recording equipment, and the action with high-speed cameras.

In the first experiments, which took place in Yack's laboratory at Carleton University, in Canada, one of the scientists simulated an attack on a caterpillar lying on a twig

The walnut sphinx caterpillar changes into a brownish pupa that then transforms into this moth. The moth lays eggs from which larvae, or caterpillars, emerge, repeating the insect's life cycle.

inside one of the experiment cages. The cage had several twigs and branches of plants familiar to the caterpillar. One of the researchers pinched the caterpillar with a blunt forceps a few times. The caterpillar was not hurt, but felt the forceps touching its body, like something was trying to grab it. When the caterpillar felt the pinch, it whistled immediately. The scientists repeated the experiment with several walnut sphinx caterpillars and obtained the same response. A threatened caterpillar whistles. But, will whistling help it escape the threat?[7]

> **Science Tongue Twisters:** **The scientific name for the North American walnut sphinx is *Amorpha juglandis*, and the yellow warbler is *Dendroica petechia*.**

To answer this question, the scientists carried out a second set of experiments that involved real attacks. At Queen's University, the scientists placed a caterpillar and a bird that hunts for caterpillars —a yellow warbler—together in the experiment cage. The microphones and cameras were on. The scientists stepped aside. After a minute or two, the bird saw the caterpillar resting on a twig. The yellow warbler approached the caterpillar and attacked it with its beak. Right away the caterpillar whistled. The bird flinched, cocked its head, looking at the caterpillar, and hopped away.[8]

"In one case, the response of the bird was dramatic," said Yack. "When the caterpillar whistled, the yellow warbler dove

Yellow warblers hunt caterpillars, but sometimes caterpillars escape by blowing a whistle that scares the birds away.

down and away from the caterpillar into thicker vegetation, as if attacked by a predator."

All the caterpillars involved in the experiments survived the attacks by yellow warblers and had no wounds from the encounters.

The Secret Is Out

Other experiments showed how caterpillars make the whistling sound. They contract some of their muscles, which pushes air out of their bodies through openings called spiracles. The air makes the spiracles vibrate, which produces the whistling sound. This was news to scientists. They knew that insects, such as crickets, make sounds by rubbing two body structures against each other. Walnut sphinx caterpillars have shown scientists that young insects can also make sounds by pushing air through body structures. Caterpillars can whistle! Yack and her colleagues have revealed the secret of the whistling caterpillars.

3

JAMMING SIGNALS, RIGHT OFF THE BAT

It looked like they were setting up for a rock concert in the middle of a field in the wild. Hours before the show, "we hauled all sorts of microphones, speakers, video cameras, and lights," said Aaron Corcoran, the leader of the team setting up for the event.[1]

The team even built towers as tall as a two-story building to set up large spotlights. They checked and rechecked that their equipment was working. When all was ready, they waited for the show to begin. As night fell, the protagonists arrived—two, three, four bats at a time.

"They zoomed after bugs and chased each other so fast we could hardly see what was going on," said Corcoran. "But my high-speed cameras and ultrasonic microphones, which are specially designed to capture fast events at night, were

In the pitch-black night, echolocation allows this bat to "see in the dark" and find a moth for food.

picking up everything. We can slow everything down when we get back to the lab."[2]

When the sun began to rise, the show was over. The bats flew back to their cave. The team packed everything and tucked themselves into bed.

Bat Chat

Aaron Corcoran, a bat biologist, learns the language of the Mexican free-tailed bat. However, Corcoran's is not an easy job. These bats live in social groups that can number in the millions. The bats chat constantly during their nocturnal outings.

They not only chat, they also use echolocation or sonar-like sounds to track prey such as moths, or find and avoid obstacles such as trees.

"Our senses are not very good for studying bats," said Corcoran. "They fly up in the air, where we cannot go, at night, when we cannot see, and make sounds we cannot hear."[3]

Luckily, new technology has come to the rescue of bat biologists. They can now use ultrasound detectors to record sounds people cannot hear and infrared high-speed cameras to see fast events at night. With the help of this technology, Corcoran has been listening into bat chats for more than ten

©WFU

Aaron Corcoran uses high-tech equipment to see, hear, and follow bats in their natural environment.

years. He and other scientists have learned that bats chat with at least fifteen calls, each with a different meaning.

"Each sound or call bats make tells us something about what bats are up to," said Corcoran. "But still we don't know what all the calls mean."[4]

One day while Corcoran was listening to one of the recordings from the field, he caught a sound he had never heard before. "Because the sound had special characteristics, I immediately thought that the bats were up to no good," Corcoran said. Intrigued, he planned a series of experiments to find out.

Jamming for Food

Corcoran suspected that the bat making the new sound was attempting to interfere with, or jam, the signals another bat was making in order to catch food. This would be like someone asking for directions to the buffet while another person was shouting to prevent the first one from hearing the directions. If the person cannot hear the location of the buffet, he or she would not be able to find it, and he would go hungry.

To test that his hypothesis was correct, Corcoran carried out his series of tests in the wild. He and his team traveled to Arizona and New Mexico, two locations where Mexican free-tailed bats live. The scientists set up ultrasound microphones, the infrared high-speed cameras, and a spotlight tower. They waited for the bats to appear.

This bat will probably catch the moth unless another bat jams its tracking signals.

Night after night, the scientists collected large amounts of data. In a first series of tests, the researchers recorded the flight paths bats had followed, their success at catching bugs, and their chats during their nocturnal foraging activities. Then, they recreated in the computer the 3-D paths the bats had flown and put it together with the calls or chats they had been making.[5]

When Corcoran and his colleagues analyzed the data, they were amazed. They realized that bats receiving the suspecting jamming calls missed catching prey more times than bats not receiving the calls. The jamming calls overlap the feeding buzz made by the receiving bat. The feeding buzz refers to very fast sounds a bat makes when it is getting close to its prey and needs to quickly get more information about the prey's exact location. Just as shouting to another person does not let him or her hear what another person is saying, jamming the feeding buzz does not let the bat know where exactly the prey is. As a result, the bat fails to catch it.

> **Science Tongue Twister**
> **The scientific name of the Mexican free-tailed bat is *Tadarida brasiliensis*.**

The scientists next tested whether playbacks of jamming calls would also make bats miss catching their prey. And they did![6]

The Hungry Bat and the Jammer

Interestingly, the story goes beyond the hungry bat and the jammer. After jamming the hungry bat, the jammer will try to catch the prey the first bat missed. But then, the bat that got jammed fights back with the same trick, shouting its own jamming calls.[7]

"This aerial duel or competition for food goes back and forth until one of them catches the prey or gives up," Corcoran said.

This discovery of bats jamming bats was a surprise.

"I can hardly believe bats are doing this," said Corcoran. "It's the first time anyone has shown animals that use echolocation 'jamming' each other. Bats are usually very good at avoiding jamming—their lives depend on it. But, in this case, bats have evolved a signal that specifically interferes with other bat's ability to 'see' around them with echolocation. I'd like to know whether other animals that use echolocation, such as other bats and some whales, do it, too."[8]

4
TALES FROM THE ZOMBIE BEETLE

A ladybug lands softly on a vibrant green leaf and folds its wings under the black-on-red spotted armor. Quietly, a green-eyed wasp approaches and circles the ladybug while swiftly feeling its body with the antennae. The wasp curves its abdomen under its body, pointing the sting toward the ladybug. It quickly pokes the ladybug's body a few times, searching for a soft spot through which it injects a single egg. Then, the wasp leaves, looking for another ladybug in which to lay another egg.

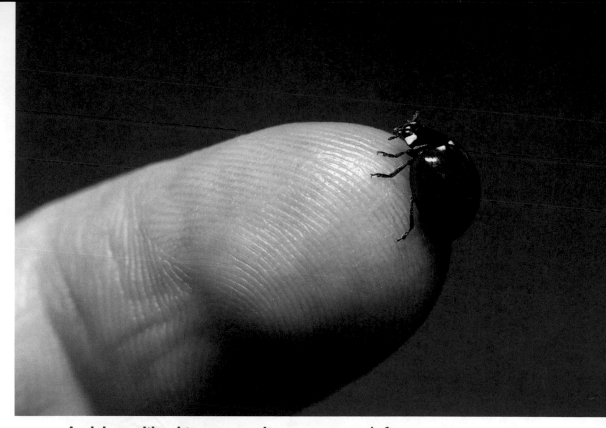

Ladybugs, like this one standing on a person's finger, can become hosts to even tinier wasp eggs.

This event marks the beginning of life for a new wasp. During the next three weeks, the wasp egg will grow into a grublike larva that feeds on the ladybug's fat. In the meantime, the ladybug goes about its normal life of feeding, flying, and running around. It is apparently unaware of the creature growing inside it.

At the end of the three weeks, the larva, which is almost as long as the ladybug's body, squeezes its way out through an opening on the ladybug's abdomen. The wormy creature remains nestled under the ladybug's legs and spins a yellowish cocoon.[1]

Green-eyed wasps look for ladybugs in which to inject their tiny eggs. This wasp is smaller than a dime.

Surprisingly, the ladybug is still very much alive. The ladybug does not abandon the cocoon. The ladybug remains on top of the cocoon until the larva has completed its transformation into a brand new wasp and leaves. Some ladybugs recover from this ordeal. They move away from the empty cocoon and continue with their lives.

Scientists wondered about the behavior of the ladybug. Why didn't it leave the cocoon to its own fate?

Ladybug Bodyguard

The ladybug did not move away from the cocoon because it was paralyzed; it could not walk, it could only twitch its legs.[2] A team of French and Canadian scientists discovered that a ladybug paralyzed on top of a wasp cocoon acts as a bodyguard for the cocoon. Cocoon predators quickly eat cocoons without ladybug bodyguards, but when a predator touches a cocoon with a ladybug on top, the ladybug twitches. The discouraged predator turns around looking for easier prey.

Most certainly, the wasp had done something to paralyze the ladybug. What could that be?

Nolwenn Dheilly took on the job of uncovering the secret of the ladybug bodyguard. Dheilly is a biologist who studies how parasites and their hosts interact with each other. She was curious about how the wasp larva, the parasite in this

A ladybug lies on top of a fuzzy wasp cocoon. Like a body-guard, the ladybug protects it from predators.

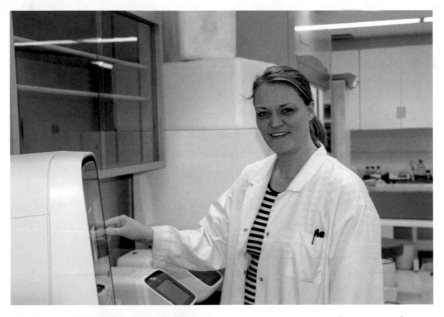

Nolwenn Dheilly uses laboratory equipment to discover the secret of the zombie beetle.

case, controls the ladybug, the host. When the ladybug is paralyzed, the wasp larva is no longer in physical contact with the ladybug; it is nestled inside the cocoon. How does it keep the bug paralyzed?[3]

An Unexpected Surprise

Dheilly suspected that when the wasp injected the egg into the ladybug, it also injected something else that damaged the nerves that help the ladybug move its legs. Maybe something in the wasp egg is toxic to the ladybug's nerves.

To find out what this "something" is, Dheilly analyzed the heads and abdomen of ladybugs after the wasp had injected its egg. She compared these analyses with those of ladybugs that had never been injected with a wasp's egg.

Dheilly found that ladybugs with a wasp larva growing inside them have a type of genetic material the healthy ladybugs don't have. Dheilly thought that this genetic material, called RNA for ribonucleic acid, must belong to the wasp. But this is not the case. The new RNA belongs to a virus nobody had seen before.[4]

"I ran around the building of my lab telling everybody that I had discovered a new viral species!" she said. "The wasp seems to use the virus as a biological weapon to control the behavior of the ladybug like a puppeteer, and make it guard the cocoon from predators. Nobody had ever shown a parasite and a virus working together like this to survive."[5]

Dheilly had the honor of naming the new virus; she called it *Dinocampus coccinellae*

WHAT IS A VIRUS?

Viruses are the smallest microbes. They can cause many diseases in people, animals, and plants. The common cold, the flu, chicken pox, and measles are a few examples of diseases caused by a virus. Viruses are very simple; they consist of a type of genetic material, either DNA or RNA, enveloped in a coat of protein. Viruses cannot make more viruses on their own; they need to enter live cells to make more viruses.

paralysis virus (DcPV). It is related to the poliovirus, which causes paralysis in people.

Timing Is Everything

Dheilly did experiments with electron microscopy to enlarge microscopic images of the insides of a wasp and a ladybug thousands of times. Using these images and other data, Dheilly figured out that the wasps inject eggs that already carry the virus. The virus invades the nerves of the ladybug. The ladybug's own body tries to get rid of the virus but, in the process, it slowly destroys nerve cells that help the ladybug move its legs.

> **Science Tongue Twisters: The scientific name of the green-eyed wasp is *Dinocampus coccinellae*. The name for ladybugs is *Colleomegilla maculata*.**

When the larva emerge and form the cocoon, the ladybug is already paralyzed. It becomes a bodyguard for the cocoon. While the cocoon grows into a fully-grown wasp, the ladybug slowly recovers the use of its legs. By the time the wasp leaves the cocoon, the ladybug can move again.[6] And in this way, Dheilly discovered the secret of the paralyzing wasp.

5
THE SECRET OF THE UNSTOPPABLE COCKROACH

Most people get rid of cockroaches as soon as they see the insects in their homes, but not Robert Full and Kaushik Jayaram, roach biologists. "We have a bucket of roaches in our lab," Full said. "Every morning we go and get a few before we begin our experiments."[1]

Full and Jayaram study how animals move. They uncover their secrets and use them to build robots that are better than the current ones.

"We look at all kinds of creatures," said Full. "We found that the strangest and ickiest ones give us the best ideas to improve robots."

The cockroach is one of these amazing creatures. Among other things, it has the impressive ability to slide through tiny cracks in a flash. Full and Jayaram were curious. How can a

Scientists study animals such as cockroaches to understand how they can run and squish through very tight spaces and to get inspiration to build better bodies for robots.

cockroach squeeze through spaces that are much smaller than the animal's body?

"They give me the shivers," Full said. "But I wanted to uncover their secret."[2]

The Surprising Cockroach

If you can get over the icky feeling, as Full and Jayaram have, take a closer look at the amazing cockroach. If you hold a cockroach in your hand beside a Skittles candy, you'll see that it is lighter than the candy. Unlike the candy, a cockroach is squishy and tough at the same time. Roaches, like people, have a skeleton, but the roach's is on the outside of the body, so it's called an exoskeleton. The exoskeleton is made of chitin, a hard material similar to keratin, from which your nails are made. The exoskeleton protects the roach's soft body parts underneath it, like a suit of armor.

Just like other insects, cockroaches have six legs that have segments with flexible joints. To know what's going on in its environment, roaches have sensors all over their bodies. The antennae can be longer than the roach's body. They let roaches know what lies ahead, such as food, predators, or a crack on the wall through which it can escape from danger.

COCKROACH SUPERPOWERS

The stiff, yet flexible, exoskeleton helps roaches run fast; in one second, a roach can distance itself 5 feet (1.5 meters) from danger. Roaches can also climb up walls, dash across ceilings, and swing under ledges.[3]

Roaches are about half an inch (thirteen millimeters) tall when they run freely but can squish their bodies to one-tenth of that size—the height of two stacked pennies—thanks in part to their tough, flexible exoskeleton.

Full and Jayaram wanted to make robots that could do some of the things roaches do, such as squeeze rapidly through tight spaces. These robots would help find survivors trapped under buildings that had collapse after earthquakes or explosions. But, before they could build their search-and-rescue robots, the scientists had to know how roach's body can squeeze and crawl through tight spaces.[4]

The Squeeze Test

"We made a little gadget that has an opening like a small window. We can make the opening narrower or wider to control the space the cockroach will slip through," said Full. "Cockroaches move too fast for the naked eye to see how they actually move their body and legs as they squeeze through tight spaces. So we surrounded the gadget with high-speed cameras to film from different angles how the cockroaches move through the window. Then, we saw the videos in slow motion."[5]

The slow-motion videos showed that roaches do not slip through tight spaces as easily as it may look at plain sight. They discovered that roaches move through in stages.

Stage 1: Explore and Detect

A cockroach in the experimental gadget immediately explored its surroundings with its long antennae. When it found a crack, it slipped the antennae through it and continued feeling its surroundings. The scientists suspect that exploring the crevice

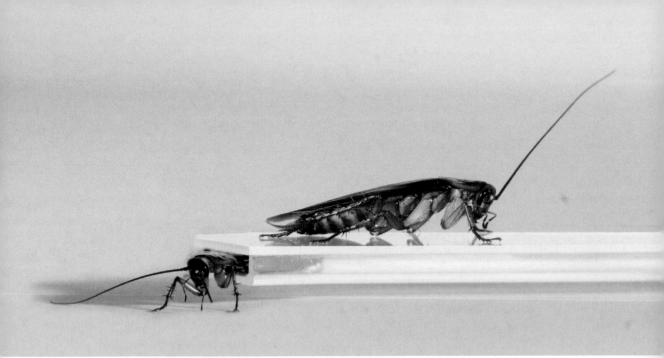

These two cockroaches are about the same size. The one on the bottom is emerging from a space only 0.2 inches (4 millimeters) wide, showing that roaches can squeeze through very tight spaces.

lets the roach know the size of the crack and whether it is safe to go through.

Stage 2: Dive Head On

After checking the opening with the antennae, the roach dove head-on through it, moving its legs rapidly, trying to grip the surfaces around it. The head and the front legs slipped thought the crack trying to pull the body through. At the same time, the roach lifted the rest of its body and pushed the surrounding walls with the middle and hind legs to get across the crevice.

Stage 3: Squeeze Through

The roach continued pushing with its hind legs and moved its body side to side as it squeezed the thorax and abdomen through the crack. The body was now flat; trapped in a tight space. The roach pushed forward, working the legs, until it was free. The wider the crevice, the quicker the cockroach went through it.[6]

Tough Roach

The scientists learned a few new, amazing things about cockroaches. Cockroaches are always fast. When a roach had plenty of room, it took about 0.3 seconds to cross the crevice. Even in the tightest spaces it took only about one second to get through! During this time the squeeze the roaches experienced was equivalent to having 300 times their body weight pressing on them.[7]

> **Science Tongue Twister**
> **The scientific name of the cockroach is *Periplaneta americana.***

"We were surprised that roaches can go through spaces that are smaller than a quarter of their height in less than a second by squeezing their flexible bodies in half!" Full said. "Once inside, they still could move forward very fast, about 1.6 yards (1.5 meters) per second. They use friction to drag their legs and body against the surface."[8]

Full and Jayaram tested the roach's toughness even further. They discovered that roaches can survive almost nine hundred times their body weight pressing on them without injury.[9]

This would be like a one hundred-pound (forty-five-kilogram) kid surviving having seven African elephants on top of him!

Roach-Inspired Robot

The cockroach has inspired Full and Jayaram to build robots that can do many of the things roaches do.

The tough cockroach inspired the scientists to build CRAM, which stands for "compressible robot with articulated mechanisms." CRAM might one day help rescue people trapped in places that are hard to reach.

"The hardest part was to understand how the roach's skeleton is put together," Full said. "How the hard, outside crunchy plates connect with each other and with the soft parts inside. Then, we had to figure out how to make the robot's body like the roach's, so it would squish without breaking as it squeezed through tight spaces. It was very difficult, but we did it!"[10]

Full and Jayaram are still making improvements to their robot. "We are closer to having a robot that can go anywhere," said Full. "Studying the cockroach's secrets will help us build robots that find people who need rescue. I believe it will happen."

HANDS-ON ACTIVITY: JAMMING MEMORIES

In this activity, you will test the effect of a distraction on a friend's ability to accomplish a task. During the first part of the experiment, your friend will carry out the activity without distractions. During the second part, you will distract your friend while he or she carries out the activity, but you will not warn your friend about the distraction.

What you need:

1. One friend
2. A stopwatch (such as the one in a cell phone)
3. A book
4. Two lists of words:
    List A: bottle, umbrella, banana, bucket, hammer, skirt, elephant, graduation, tornado, submarine
    List B: glass, suitcase, apple, sunglasses, scissors, jacket, mosquito, birthday, hurricane, airplane
5. A piece of paper
6. A pencil

What to do:

1. Ask a friend to help you do the experiment.
2. Give your friend list A of words (with the sheet turned face down), a blank sheet of paper, and a pencil.

3. Instruct your friend that, on your mark, he or she will have twenty seconds to memorize the words on the list. At the end of the twenty seconds, your friend will have twenty seconds to write the words he or she remembers on the piece of paper.

4. Set the stopwatch for twenty seconds and give your friend a go to begin memorizing the words.

5. At the end of twenty seconds, take the list, set the stopwatch for twenty seconds more, and tell your friend to write the words he or she remembers on the paper. At the end of the twenty seconds, instruct your friend to stop writing.

6. Tell your friend that you will repeat the experiment with a new list of words (List B). (Do not warn your friend that you plan to distract him or her.)

7. Set the stopwatch for twenty seconds and give your friend a go to begin memorizing the words.

8. As the twenty seconds begin, stand by your friend and read aloud (really loud!) from your book. Do not stop regardless of what your friend might do.

9. At the end of twenty seconds, take the list, set the stopwatch for twenty seconds, and tell your friend to write the words he or she remembers on the paper. At the end of the twenty seconds, instruct your friend to stop writing.

Results:

1. How many words did your friend remember the first time you did the experiment?

2. How many words did your friend remember the second time?

3. Was your "jamming" effective at blocking your friend's ability to memorize words?

4. Repeat the experiment with new lists of ten words, and change the memorizing and recall times to sixty seconds. Does a longer time make it easier to memorize and recall the words?

★ CHAPTER NOTES ★

Chapter 1: The Secret of the Scuba Diving Spider

1. Dr. Roger Seymour, email interview with author, January 2, 2017.
2. Kathryn Knight, "How the Water Spider Uses its Diving Bell," *Inside JEB*, July 1, 2011, doi: 10.1242/jeb.060731.
3. Dr. Seymour.
4. Ibid.
5. Roger S. Seymour, Stefan K. Hetz, "The Diving Bell and the Spider: the Physical Gill of *Argyroneta aquatica*," *The Journal of Experimental Medicine*, vol. 214, 2011, p.2175.
6. Dr. Seymour.
7. Seymour and Hetz, p. 2175.
8. Ibid., p. 2181.
9. Dr. Seymour.

Chapter 2: A Caterpillar's Emergency Whistle

1. Dr. Jayne Yack, email interview with author, December 6, 2016.
2. Jayne Yack, Myron Smith, and Patrick Weatherhead, "Caterpillar talk: Acoustically mediated territoriality in larval Lepidoptera," *Proceedings of the National Academy of Sciences*, vol. 98, 2001, p.11371.
3. Dr. Yack.
4. Veronica L. Bura , Vanya Rohwer , Paul Martin and Jayne Yack, "Whistling in caterpillars (*Amorpha juglandis*, Bombycoidea): sound-producing mechanism and function," *The Journal of Experimental Biology*, vol 214, 2011,p. 30.
5. Ibid., p. 30.
6. Ibid., p. 31.
7. Ibid., p. 33.
8. Ibid., p. 34.

44

Chapter 3: Jamming Signals, Right Off the Bat

1. Dr. Aaron Corcoran, email interview with author, December 13, 2016.
2. Ibid.
3. Ibid.
4. Ibid.
5. Aaron Corcoran and William Conner, "Bats jamming bats: Food competition through sonar interference," *Science*, vol. 346, 2014, p.745.
6. Corcoran and Conner.
7. Ibid.

Chapter 4: Tales from the Zombie Beetle

1. Nolwenn M. Dheilly et al., "Who is the puppet master? Replication of a parasitic wasp-associated virus correlates with host behaviour manipulation," *Proceedings of the Royal Society B*, vol. 282, 2015: 20142773, p.1. http://dx.doi.org/10.1098/rspb.2014.2773
2. Dheilly et al., p.2.
3. Phone interview with Dr. Nolwenn Dheilly, October 26, 2016.
4. Dheilly et al., p.3.
5. Dr. Dheilly.
6. Dheilly et al., p.8.

Chapter 5: The Secret of the Unstoppable Cockroach

1. Dr. Robert Full, phone interview with author, October 26, 2016.
2. Ibid.
3. Kaushik Jayaram and Robert J. Full, "Cockroaches traverse crevices, crawl rapidly in confined spaces, and inspire a soft, legged robot," *Proceedings of the National Academy of Sciences*, vol. 113, 2016, p. E950.
4. Dr. Full.
5. Ibid.
6. Jayaram and Full, p. E952.
7. Ibid., p. E952.
8. Dr. Full.
9. Jayaram and Full, p. E956.
10. Dr. Full.

★ GLOSSARY ★

arthropods ★ An invertebrate animal that has jointed limbs, a segmented body, and an exoskeleton made of chitin.

chitin ★ A tough semitransparent coating that protects the outside body of some insects.

cocoon ★ The silky covering that encloses a caterpillar while it transforms into an adult.

diving bell ★ A chamber that holds air underwater.

electron microscope ★ A microscope that uses beams of electrons instead of light to make small objects look bigger.

exoskeleton ★ A hard, external protective covering of some organisms, such as insects.

forceps ★ A surgical instrument with two parts that move together like chopsticks to hold something.

gill ★ A breathing organ of a fish that allows oxygen dissolved in water to pass into the organism.

keratin ★ The main protein that makes up hair, nails, feathers, and hooves.

mandible ★ The mouth part of an insect.

nerve ★ Fibers of the nervous system that carry messages between the brain or the spinal cord and organs of the body.

optode ★ A sensor to detect chemicals, such as oxygen.

pollution ★ Contamination of the environment.

predator ★ An animal that hunts other animals for food.

spiracle ★ A small opening in an insect.

toxic ★ Poisonous.

ultrasonic ★ Sound people cannot hear.

vegetation ★ Plants growing in a particular place.

virus ★ A microscopic particle that can replicate inside living cells.

★ FURTHER READING ★

Books

Bishop, Nic. *Spiders*. New York, NY: Scholastic, 2014.

De la Bedoyere, Camilla. *Caterpillar to Butterfly*. London, UK: QED Publishing, 2016.

Markle, Sandra. *The Case of the Vanishing Little Brown Bats: A Scientific Mystery*. Minneapolis, MN: Millbrook Press, 2014.

Nelson, Robin. *Crawling Cockroaches*. Minneapolis, MN: Lerner Publications, 2016.

Websites

PBS Digital Studios: It's OKAY to Be Smart
youtube.com/watch?v=P_tykwBvqZ0

Watch an educational video about bats, guardians of the night.

The University of California at Berkeley, Museum of Paleontology
evolution.berkeley.edu/evolibrary/article/arthropods_06

Learn more about the science of an exoskeleton.

★ INDEX ★